To:

_____

From:

_____

Date:

_____

_____

_____

_____

_____

_____

_____

_____

_____

_____

_____

_____

_____

_____

_____

_____

_____

_____

_____

_____

_____

_____

_____

DELIGHT YOURSELF IN THE LORD,
AND HE WILL GIVE YOU THE DESIRES OF YOUR HEART.

PSALM 37:4

THE LORD IS MY LIGHT AND MY SALVATION—
WHOM SHALL I FEAR? THE LORD IS THE STRONGHOLD OF
MY LIFE—OF WHOM SHALL I BE AFRAID? PSALM 27:1

THE LORD HIMSELF GOES BEFORE YOU AND WILL BE WITH YOU;
HE WILL NEVER LEAVE YOU NOR FORSAKE YOU.

DEUTERONOMY 31:8

GOD IS WORKING IN YOU, GIVING YOU THE DESIRE
TO OBEY HIM AND THE POWER TO DO WHAT PLEASES HIM.

PHILIPPIANS 2:13

I CAN DO EVERYTHING THROUGH CHRIST, WHO GIVES ME STRENGTH.

PHILIPPIANS 4:13

IF YOU WANT TO KNOW WHAT GOD WANTS YOU TO DO,
ASK HIM, AND HE WILL GLADLY TELL YOU.

JAMES 1:5

CREATE IN ME A PURE HEART, O GOD,
AND RENEW A STEADFAST SPIRIT WITHIN ME.

PSALM 51:10

IF ANYONE IS IN CHRIST, THE NEW CREATION HAS COME:
THE OLD HAS GONE, THE NEW IS HERE!

2 CORINTHIANS 5:17

CAST YOUR CARES ON THE LORD AND HE WILL SUSTAIN YOU.

PSALM 55:22

THE LORD YOUR GOD IS WITH YOU, THE MIGHTY WARRIOR WHO SAVES. HE WILL
TAKE GREAT DELIGHT IN YOU; IN HIS LOVE HE WILL NO LONGER REBUKE YOU.

THE LORD IS TRUSTWORTHY IN ALL HE
PROMISES AND FAITHFUL IN ALL HE DOES.

PSALM 145:13

IN YOU, O LORD, DO I TAKE REFUGE;
LET ME NEVER BE PUT TO SHAME!

PSALM 71:1

_____

_____

_____

_____

_____

_____

_____

_____

_____

_____

_____

_____

_____

_____

_____

_____

_____

_____

_____

_____

_____

_____

_____

_____

_____

"BE STRONG AND COURAGEOUS . . . THE LORD YOUR GOD
WILL BE WITH YOU WHEREVER YOU GO."

JOSHUA 1:9

COMMIT TO THE LORD WHATEVER YOU DO,
AND HE WILL ESTABLISH YOUR PLANS.

PROVERBS 16:3

SINCE WE HAVE BEEN JUSTIFIED THROUGH FAITH,
WE HAVE PEACE WITH GOD THROUGH OUR LORD JESUS CHRIST.

ROMANS 5:1

_____

_____

_____

_____

_____

_____

_____

_____

_____

_____

_____

_____

_____

_____

_____

_____

_____

_____

_____

_____

_____

_____

_____

_____

THE LORD IS MY ROCK, MY FORTRESS AND MY DELIVERER;
MY GOD IS MY ROCK, IN WHOM I TAKE REFUGE.

PSALM 18:2

_____

_____

_____

_____

_____

_____

_____

_____

_____

_____

_____

_____

_____

_____

_____

_____

_____

_____

_____

_____

_____

_____

_____

"IF ANYONE WOULD COME AFTER ME, LET HIM DENY HIMSELF
AND TAKE UP HIS CROSS AND FOLLOW ME."

MATTHEW 16:24

THE WORD OF THE LORD IS RIGHT AND TRUE;
HE IS FAITHFUL IN ALL HE DOES.

THE LORD IS MY STRENGTH AND MY SHIELD;
MY HEART TRUSTS IN HIM, AND HE HELPS ME.

IN HIM WE HAVE REDEMPTION THROUGH HIS BLOOD,
THE FORGIVENESS OF SINS, IN ACCORDANCE
WITH THE RICHES OF GOD'S GRACE. EPHESIANS 1:7

I TRUST IN YOUR UNFAILING LOVE. I WILL REJOICE
BECAUSE YOU HAVE RESCUED ME. I WILL SING TO
THE LORD BECAUSE HE IS SO GOOD TO ME. PSALM 13:5-6

WALK IN THE WAY OF LOVE, JUST AS CHRIST LOVED US
AND GAVE HIMSELF UP FOR US AS A FRAGRANT
OFFERING AND SACRIFICE TO GOD. EPHESIANS 5:2

_____

_____

_____

_____

_____

_____

_____

_____

_____

_____

_____

_____

_____

_____

_____

_____

_____

_____

_____

_____

_____

_____

_____

"YOU WILL CALL UPON ME AND COME AND PRAY TO ME, AND I WILL
LISTEN TO YOU. YOU WILL SEEK ME AND FIND ME WHEN
YOU SEEK ME WITH ALL YOUR HEART." JEREMIAH 29:12-13

MY SOUL FINDS REST IN GOD; MY SALVATION COMES FROM HIM.

_____

_____

_____

_____

_____

_____

_____

_____

_____

_____

_____

_____

_____

_____

_____

_____

_____

_____

_____

_____

_____

_____

DELIGHT YOURSELF IN THE LORD,
AND HE WILL GIVE YOU THE DESIRES OF YOUR HEART.

PSALM 37:4

THE LORD IS MY LIGHT AND MY SALVATION—
WHOM SHALL I FEAR? THE LORD IS THE STRONGHOLD OF
MY LIFE—OF WHOM SHALL I BE AFRAID? PSALM 27:1

THE LORD HIMSELF GOES BEFORE YOU AND WILL BE WITH YOU;
HE WILL NEVER LEAVE YOU NOR FORSAKE YOU.

DEUTERONOMY 31:8

GOD IS WORKING IN YOU, GIVING YOU THE DESIRE
TO OBEY HIM AND THE POWER TO DO WHAT PLEASES HIM.

PHILIPPIANS 2:13

I CAN DO EVERYTHING THROUGH CHRIST, WHO GIVES ME STRENGTH.

IF YOU WANT TO KNOW WHAT GOD WANTS YOU TO DO,
ASK HIM, AND HE WILL GLADLY TELL YOU.

JAMES 1:5

CREATE IN ME A PURE HEART, O GOD,
AND RENEW A STEADFAST SPIRIT WITHIN ME.

PSALM 51:10

IF ANYONE IS IN CHRIST, THE NEW CREATION HAS COME:
THE OLD HAS GONE, THE NEW IS HERE!

2 CORINTHIANS 5:17

CAST YOUR CARES ON THE LORD AND HE WILL SUSTAIN YOU.

THE LORD YOUR GOD IS WITH YOU, THE MIGHTY WARRIOR WHO SAVES. HE WILL
TAKE GREAT DELIGHT IN YOU; IN HIS LOVE HE WILL NO LONGER REBUKE YOU.

THE LORD IS TRUSTWORTHY IN ALL HE
PROMISES AND FAITHFUL IN ALL HE DOES.

PSALM 145:13

IN YOU, O LORD, DO I TAKE REFUGE;
LET ME NEVER BE PUT TO SHAME!

PSALM 71:1

_____

_____

_____

_____

_____

_____

_____

_____

_____

_____

_____

_____

_____

_____

_____

_____

_____

_____

_____

_____

_____

_____

_____

"BE STRONG AND COURAGEOUS . . . THE LORD YOUR GOD
WILL BE WITH YOU WHEREVER YOU GO."

JOSHUA 1:9

COMMIT TO THE LORD WHATEVER YOU DO,
AND HE WILL ESTABLISH YOUR PLANS.

PROVERBS 16:3

SINCE WE HAVE BEEN JUSTIFIED THROUGH FAITH,
WE HAVE PEACE WITH GOD THROUGH OUR LORD JESUS CHRIST.

ROMANS 5:1

THE LORD IS MY ROCK, MY FORTRESS AND MY DELIVERER;
MY GOD IS MY ROCK, IN WHOM I TAKE REFUGE.

PSALM 18:2

"IF ANYONE WOULD COME AFTER ME, LET HIM DENY HIMSELF
AND TAKE UP HIS CROSS AND FOLLOW ME."

MATTHEW 16:24

_____

_____

_____

_____

_____

_____

_____

_____

_____

_____

_____

_____

_____

_____

_____

_____

_____

_____

_____

_____

_____

_____

_____

_____

THE WORD OF THE LORD IS RIGHT AND TRUE;
HE IS FAITHFUL IN ALL HE DOES.

PSALM 33:4

THE LORD IS MY STRENGTH AND MY SHIELD;
MY HEART TRUSTS IN HIM, AND HE HELPS ME.

PSALM 28:7

IN HIM WE HAVE REDEMPTION THROUGH HIS BLOOD,
THE FORGIVENESS OF SINS, IN ACCORDANCE
WITH THE RICHES OF GOD'S GRACE. EPHESIANS 1:7

I TRUST IN YOUR UNFAILING LOVE. I WILL REJOICE
BECAUSE YOU HAVE RESCUED ME. I WILL SING TO
THE LORD BECAUSE HE IS SO GOOD TO ME. PSALM 13:5-6

WALK IN THE WAY OF LOVE, JUST AS CHRIST LOVED US
AND GAVE HIMSELF UP FOR US AS A FRAGRANT
OFFERING AND SACRIFICE TO GOD. EPHESIANS 5:2

_____

_____

_____

_____

_____

_____

_____

_____

_____

_____

_____

_____

_____

_____

_____

_____

_____

_____

_____

_____

_____

_____

_____

_____

"YOU WILL CALL UPON ME AND COME AND PRAY TO ME, AND I WILL
LISTEN TO YOU. YOU WILL SEEK ME AND FIND ME WHEN
YOU SEEK ME WITH ALL YOUR HEART." JEREMIAH 29:12-13

MY SOUL FINDS REST IN GOD; MY SALVATION COMES FROM HIM.

PSALM 62:1

DELIGHT YOURSELF IN THE LORD,
AND HE WILL GIVE YOU THE DESIRES OF YOUR HEART.

PSALM 37:4

THE LORD IS MY LIGHT AND MY SALVATION—
WHOM SHALL I FEAR? THE LORD IS THE STRONGHOLD OF
MY LIFE—OF WHOM SHALL I BE AFRAID? PSALM 27:1

THE LORD HIMSELF GOES BEFORE YOU AND WILL BE WITH YOU;
HE WILL NEVER LEAVE YOU NOR FORSAKE YOU.

DEUTERONOMY 31:8

GOD IS WORKING IN YOU, GIVING YOU THE DESIRE
TO OBEY HIM AND THE POWER TO DO WHAT PLEASES HIM.

PHILIPPIANS 2:13

I CAN DO EVERYTHING THROUGH CHRIST, WHO GIVES ME STRENGTH.

PHILIPPIANS 4:13

_____

_____

_____

_____

_____

_____

_____

_____

_____

_____

_____

_____

_____

_____

_____

_____

_____

_____

_____

_____

IF YOU WANT TO KNOW WHAT GOD WANTS YOU TO DO,
ASK HIM, AND HE WILL GLADLY TELL YOU.

JAMES 1:5

CREATE IN ME A PURE HEART, O GOD,
AND RENEW A STEADFAST SPIRIT WITHIN ME.

PSALM 51:10

_____

_____

_____

_____

_____

_____

_____

_____

_____

_____

_____

_____

_____

_____

_____

_____

_____

_____

_____

_____

_____

_____

_____

_____

IF ANYONE IS IN CHRIST, THE NEW CREATION HAS COME:
THE OLD HAS GONE, THE NEW IS HERE!

2 CORINTHIANS 5:17

CAST YOUR CARES ON THE LORD AND HE WILL SUSTAIN YOU.

_____

_____

_____

_____

_____

_____

_____

_____

_____

_____

_____

_____

_____

_____

_____

_____

_____

_____

_____

_____

_____

_____

_____

_____

THE LORD YOUR GOD IS WITH YOU, THE MIGHTY WARRIOR WHO SAVES. HE WILL
TAKE GREAT DELIGHT IN YOU; IN HIS LOVE HE WILL NO LONGER REBUKE YOU.

ZEPHANIAH 3:17

THE LORD IS TRUSTWORTHY IN ALL HE
PROMISES AND FAITHFUL IN ALL HE DOES.

PSALM 145:13

IN YOU, O LORD, DO I TAKE REFUGE;
LET ME NEVER BE PUT TO SHAME!

PSALM 71:1

_____

_____

_____

_____

_____

_____

_____

_____

_____

_____

_____

_____

_____

_____

_____

_____

_____

_____

_____

_____

_____

_____

"BE STRONG AND COURAGEOUS . . . THE LORD YOUR GOD
WILL BE WITH YOU WHEREVER YOU GO."

JOSHUA 1:9

COMMIT TO THE LORD WHATEVER YOU DO,
AND HE WILL ESTABLISH YOUR PLANS.

PROVERBS 16:3

_____

_____

_____

_____

_____

_____

_____

_____

_____

_____

_____

_____

_____

_____

_____

_____

_____

_____

_____

_____

_____

_____

_____

SINCE WE HAVE BEEN JUSTIFIED THROUGH FAITH,
WE HAVE PEACE WITH GOD THROUGH OUR LORD JESUS CHRIST.

ROMANS 5:1

THE LORD IS MY ROCK, MY FORTRESS AND MY DELIVERER;
MY GOD IS MY ROCK, IN WHOM I TAKE REFUGE.

PSALM 18:2

"IF ANYONE WOULD COME AFTER ME, LET HIM DENY HIMSELF
AND TAKE UP HIS CROSS AND FOLLOW ME."

MATTHEW 16:24

_____

_____

_____

_____

_____

_____

_____

_____

_____

_____

_____

_____

_____

_____

_____

_____

_____

_____

_____

_____

_____

THE WORD OF THE LORD IS RIGHT AND TRUE;
HE IS FAITHFUL IN ALL HE DOES.

PSALM 33:4

THE LORD IS MY STRENGTH AND MY SHIELD;
MY HEART TRUSTS IN HIM, AND HE HELPS ME.

_____

_____

_____

_____

_____

_____

_____

_____

_____

_____

_____

_____

_____

_____

_____

_____

_____

_____

_____

_____

_____

_____

_____

IN HIM WE HAVE REDEMPTION THROUGH HIS BLOOD,
THE FORGIVENESS OF SINS, IN ACCORDANCE
WITH THE RICHES OF GOD'S GRACE. EPHESIANS 1:7

_____

_____

_____

_____

_____

_____

_____

_____

_____

_____

_____

_____

_____

_____

_____

_____

_____

_____

_____

_____

_____

_____

_____

_____

I TRUST IN YOUR UNFAILING LOVE. I WILL REJOICE
BECAUSE YOU HAVE RESCUED ME. I WILL SING TO
THE LORD BECAUSE HE IS SO GOOD TO ME. PSALM 13:5-6

WALK IN THE WAY OF LOVE, JUST AS CHRIST LOVED US
AND GAVE HIMSELF UP FOR US AS A FRAGRANT
OFFERING AND SACRIFICE TO GOD. EPHESIANS 5:2

_____

_____

_____

_____

_____

_____

_____

_____

_____

_____

_____

_____

_____

_____

_____

_____

_____

_____

_____

_____

_____

_____

_____

"YOU WILL CALL UPON ME AND COME AND PRAY TO ME, AND I WILL
LISTEN TO YOU. YOU WILL SEEK ME AND FIND ME WHEN
YOU SEEK ME WITH ALL YOUR HEART." JEREMIAH 29:12-13

_____

_____

_____

_____

_____

_____

_____

_____

_____

_____

_____

_____

_____

_____

_____

_____

_____

_____

_____

_____

_____

_____

MY SOUL FINDS REST IN GOD; MY SALVATION COMES FROM HIM.

PSALM 62:1

_____

_____

_____

_____

_____

_____

_____

_____

_____

_____

_____

_____

_____

_____

_____

_____

_____

_____

_____

_____

_____

_____

_____

DELIGHT YOURSELF IN THE LORD,
AND HE WILL GIVE YOU THE DESIRES OF YOUR HEART.

PSALM 37:4

THE LORD IS MY LIGHT AND MY SALVATION—
WHOM SHALL I FEAR? THE LORD IS THE STRONGHOLD OF
MY LIFE—OF WHOM SHALL I BE AFRAID? PSALM 27:1

_____

_____

_____

_____

_____

_____

_____

_____

_____

_____

_____

_____

_____

_____

_____

_____

_____

_____

_____

_____

THE LORD HIMSELF GOES BEFORE YOU AND WILL BE WITH YOU;
HE WILL NEVER LEAVE YOU NOR FORSAKE YOU.

DEUTERONOMY 31:8

GOD IS WORKING IN YOU, GIVING YOU THE DESIRE
TO OBEY HIM AND THE POWER TO DO WHAT PLEASES HIM.

PHILIPPIANS 2:13

I CAN DO EVERYTHING THROUGH CHRIST, WHO GIVES ME STRENGTH.

PHILIPPIANS 4:13

IF YOU WANT TO KNOW WHAT GOD WANTS YOU TO DO,
ASK HIM, AND HE WILL GLADLY TELL YOU.

JAMES 1:5

CREATE IN ME A PURE HEART, O GOD,
AND RENEW A STEADFAST SPIRIT WITHIN ME.

PSALM 51:10

IF ANYONE IS IN CHRIST, THE NEW CREATION HAS COME:
THE OLD HAS GONE, THE NEW IS HERE!

2 CORINTHIANS 5:17

CAST YOUR CARES ON THE LORD AND HE WILL SUSTAIN YOU.

THE LORD YOUR GOD IS WITH YOU, THE MIGHTY WARRIOR WHO SAVES. HE WILL
TAKE GREAT DELIGHT IN YOU; IN HIS LOVE HE WILL NO LONGER REBUKE YOU.

ZEPHANIAH 3:17

THE LORD IS TRUSTWORTHY IN ALL HE
PROMISES AND FAITHFUL IN ALL HE DOES.

PSALM 145:13

IN YOU, O LORD, DO I TAKE REFUGE;
LET ME NEVER BE PUT TO SHAME!

PSALM 71:1

_____

_____

_____

_____

_____

_____

_____

_____

_____

_____

_____

_____

_____

_____

_____

_____

_____

_____

_____

_____

_____

_____

**"BE STRONG AND COURAGEOUS . . . THE LORD YOUR GOD
WILL BE WITH YOU WHEREVER YOU GO."**

JOSHUA 1:9

COMMIT TO THE LORD WHATEVER YOU DO,
AND HE WILL ESTABLISH YOUR PLANS.

PROVERBS 16:3

SINCE WE HAVE BEEN JUSTIFIED THROUGH FAITH,
WE HAVE PEACE WITH GOD THROUGH OUR LORD JESUS CHRIST.

ROMANS 5:1

THE LORD IS MY ROCK, MY FORTRESS AND MY DELIVERER;
MY GOD IS MY ROCK, IN WHOM I TAKE REFUGE.

PSALM 18:2

"IF ANYONE WOULD COME AFTER ME, LET HIM DENY HIMSELF
AND TAKE UP HIS CROSS AND FOLLOW ME."

MATTHEW 16:24

_____

_____

_____

_____

_____

_____

_____

_____

_____

_____

_____

_____

_____

_____

_____

_____

_____

_____

_____

_____

_____

_____

THE WORD OF THE LORD IS RIGHT AND TRUE;
HE IS FAITHFUL IN ALL HE DOES.

PSALM 33:4

THE LORD IS MY STRENGTH AND MY SHIELD;
MY HEART TRUSTS IN HIM, AND HE HELPS ME.

_____

_____

_____

_____

_____

_____

_____

_____

_____

_____

_____

_____

_____

_____

_____

_____

_____

_____

_____

_____

_____

_____

IN HIM WE HAVE REDEMPTION THROUGH HIS BLOOD,
THE FORGIVENESS OF SINS, IN ACCORDANCE
WITH THE RICHES OF GOD'S GRACE. EPHESIANS 1:7

_____

_____

_____

_____

_____

_____

_____

_____

_____

_____

_____

_____

_____

_____

_____

_____

_____

_____

_____

_____

_____

_____

I TRUST IN YOUR UNFAILING LOVE. I WILL REJOICE
BECAUSE YOU HAVE RESCUED ME. I WILL SING TO
THE LORD BECAUSE HE IS SO GOOD TO ME. PSALM 13:5-6

WALK IN THE WAY OF LOVE, JUST AS CHRIST LOVED US
AND GAVE HIMSELF UP FOR US AS A FRAGRANT
OFFERING AND SACRIFICE TO GOD. EPHESIANS 5:2

"YOU WILL CALL UPON ME AND COME AND PRAY TO ME, AND I WILL
LISTEN TO YOU. YOU WILL SEEK ME AND FIND ME WHEN
YOU SEEK ME WITH ALL YOUR HEART." JEREMIAH 29:12-13

MY SOUL FINDS REST IN GOD; MY SALVATION COMES FROM HIM.

PSALM 62:1

DELIGHT YOURSELF IN THE LORD,
AND HE WILL GIVE YOU THE DESIRES OF YOUR HEART.

PSALM 37:4

THE LORD IS MY LIGHT AND MY SALVATION—
WHOM SHALL I FEAR? THE LORD IS THE STRONGHOLD OF
MY LIFE—OF WHOM SHALL I BE AFRAID? PSALM 27:1

THE LORD HIMSELF GOES BEFORE YOU AND WILL BE WITH YOU;
HE WILL NEVER LEAVE YOU NOR FORSAKE YOU.

DEUTERONOMY 31:8

_____

_____

_____

_____

_____

_____

_____

_____

_____

_____

_____

_____

_____

_____

_____

_____

_____

_____

_____

_____

_____

GOD IS WORKING IN YOU, GIVING YOU THE DESIRE
TO OBEY HIM AND THE POWER TO DO WHAT PLEASES HIM.

PHILIPPIANS 2:13

_____

_____

_____

_____

_____

_____

_____

_____

_____

_____

_____

_____

_____

_____

_____

_____

_____

_____

_____

_____

_____

_____

_____

_____

I CAN DO EVERYTHING THROUGH CHRIST, WHO GIVES ME STRENGTH.

PHILIPPIANS 4:13

IF YOU WANT TO KNOW WHAT GOD WANTS YOU TO DO,
ASK HIM, AND HE WILL GLADLY TELL YOU.

JAMES 1:5

CREATE IN ME A PURE HEART, O GOD,
AND RENEW A STEADFAST SPIRIT WITHIN ME.

PSALM 51:10

IF ANYONE IS IN CHRIST, THE NEW CREATION HAS COME:
THE OLD HAS GONE, THE NEW IS HERE!

2 CORINTHIANS 5:17

CAST YOUR CARES ON THE LORD AND HE WILL SUSTAIN YOU.

PSALM 55:22

THE LORD YOUR GOD IS WITH YOU, THE MIGHTY WARRIOR WHO SAVES. HE WILL
TAKE GREAT DELIGHT IN YOU; IN HIS LOVE HE WILL NO LONGER REBUKE YOU.

THE LORD IS TRUSTWORTHY IN ALL HE
PROMISES AND FAITHFUL IN ALL HE DOES.

PSALM 145:13

IN YOU, O LORD, DO I TAKE REFUGE;
LET ME NEVER BE PUT TO SHAME!

PSALM 71:1

"BE STRONG AND COURAGEOUS . . . THE LORD YOUR GOD
WILL BE WITH YOU WHEREVER YOU GO."

JOSHUA 1:9

COMMIT TO THE LORD WHATEVER YOU DO,
AND HE WILL ESTABLISH YOUR PLANS.

PROVERBS 16:3

SINCE WE HAVE BEEN JUSTIFIED THROUGH FAITH,
WE HAVE PEACE WITH GOD THROUGH OUR LORD JESUS CHRIST.

ROMANS 5:1

THE LORD IS MY ROCK, MY FORTRESS AND MY DELIVERER;
MY GOD IS MY ROCK, IN WHOM I TAKE REFUGE.

PSALM 18:2

_____

_____

_____

_____

_____

_____

_____

_____

_____

_____

_____

_____

_____

_____

_____

_____

_____

_____

_____

_____

_____

_____

_____

"IF ANYONE WOULD COME AFTER ME, LET HIM DENY HIMSELF
AND TAKE UP HIS CROSS AND FOLLOW ME."

MATTHEW 16:24

THE WORD OF THE LORD IS RIGHT AND TRUE;
HE IS FAITHFUL IN ALL HE DOES.

PSALM 33:4

THE LORD IS MY STRENGTH AND MY SHIELD;
MY HEART TRUSTS IN HIM, AND HE HELPS ME.

PSALM 28:7

IN HIM WE HAVE REDEMPTION THROUGH HIS BLOOD,
THE FORGIVENESS OF SINS, IN ACCORDANCE
WITH THE RICHES OF GOD'S GRACE. EPHESIANS 1:7

_____

_____

_____

_____

_____

_____

_____

_____

_____

_____

_____

_____

_____

_____

_____

_____

_____

_____

_____

_____

_____

I TRUST IN YOUR UNFAILING LOVE. I WILL REJOICE
BECAUSE YOU HAVE RESCUED ME. I WILL SING TO
THE LORD BECAUSE HE IS SO GOOD TO ME. PSALM 13:5-6

WALK IN THE WAY OF LOVE, JUST AS CHRIST LOVED US
AND GAVE HIMSELF UP FOR US AS A FRAGRANT
OFFERING AND SACRIFICE TO GOD. EPHESIANS 5:2

_____

_____

_____

_____

_____

_____

_____

_____

_____

_____

_____

_____

_____

_____

_____

_____

_____

_____

_____

_____

_____

_____

_____

_____

_____

"YOU WILL CALL UPON ME AND COME AND PRAY TO ME, AND I WILL
LISTEN TO YOU. YOU WILL SEEK ME AND FIND ME WHEN
YOU SEEK ME WITH ALL YOUR HEART." JEREMIAH 29:12-13

MY SOUL FINDS REST IN GOD; MY SALVATION COMES FROM HIM.

PSALM 62:1

_____

_____

_____

_____

_____

_____

_____

_____

_____

_____

_____

_____

_____

_____

_____

_____

_____

_____

_____

_____

_____

_____

_____

DELIGHT YOURSELF IN THE LORD,
AND HE WILL GIVE YOU THE DESIRES OF YOUR HEART.

PSALM 37:4

THE LORD IS MY LIGHT AND MY SALVATION—
WHOM SHALL I FEAR? THE LORD IS THE STRONGHOLD OF
MY LIFE—OF WHOM SHALL I BE AFRAID? PSALM 27:1

THE LORD HIMSELF GOES BEFORE YOU AND WILL BE WITH YOU;
HE WILL NEVER LEAVE YOU NOR FORSAKE YOU.

DEUTERONOMY 31:8

_____

_____

_____

_____

_____

_____

_____

_____

_____

_____

_____

_____

_____

_____

_____

_____

_____

_____

_____

_____

_____

_____

_____

_____

GOD IS WORKING IN YOU, GIVING YOU THE DESIRE
TO OBEY HIM AND THE POWER TO DO WHAT PLEASES HIM.

PHILIPPIANS 2:13

I CAN DO EVERYTHING THROUGH CHRIST, WHO GIVES ME STRENGTH.

PHILIPPIANS 4:13

_____

_____

_____

_____

_____

_____

_____

_____

_____

_____

_____

_____

_____

_____

_____

_____

_____

_____

_____

_____

_____

_____

_____

_____

IF YOU WANT TO KNOW WHAT GOD WANTS YOU TO DO,
ASK HIM, AND HE WILL GLADLY TELL YOU.

JAMES 1:5

CREATE IN ME A PURE HEART, O GOD,
AND RENEW A STEADFAST SPIRIT WITHIN ME.

PSALM 51:10

_____

_____

_____

_____

_____

_____

_____

_____

_____

_____

_____

_____

_____

_____

_____

_____

_____

_____

_____

_____

_____

_____

_____

IF ANYONE IS IN CHRIST, THE NEW CREATION HAS COME:
THE OLD HAS GONE, THE NEW IS HERE!

2 CORINTHIANS 5:17

CAST YOUR CARES ON THE LORD AND HE WILL SUSTAIN YOU.

PSALM 55:22

THE LORD YOUR GOD IS WITH YOU, THE MIGHTY WARRIOR WHO SAVES. HE WILL
TAKE GREAT DELIGHT IN YOU; IN HIS LOVE HE WILL NO LONGER REBUKE YOU.

ZEPHANIAH 3:17

THE LORD IS TRUSTWORTHY IN ALL HE
PROMISES AND FAITHFUL IN ALL HE DOES.

PSALM 145:13

IN YOU, O LORD, DO I TAKE REFUGE;
LET ME NEVER BE PUT TO SHAME!

PSALM 71:1

_____

_____

_____

_____

_____

_____

_____

_____

_____

_____

_____

_____

_____

_____

_____

_____

_____

_____

_____

_____

_____

_____

"BE STRONG AND COURAGEOUS . . . THE LORD YOUR GOD
WILL BE WITH YOU WHEREVER YOU GO."

JOSHUA 1:9

COMMIT TO THE LORD WHATEVER YOU DO,
AND HE WILL ESTABLISH YOUR PLANS.

PROVERBS 16:3

SINCE WE HAVE BEEN JUSTIFIED THROUGH FAITH,
WE HAVE PEACE WITH GOD THROUGH OUR LORD JESUS CHRIST.

ROMANS 5:1

THE LORD IS MY ROCK, MY FORTRESS AND MY DELIVERER;
MY GOD IS MY ROCK, IN WHOM I TAKE REFUGE.

PSALM 18:2

_____

_____

_____

_____

_____

_____

_____

_____

_____

_____

_____

_____

_____

_____

_____

_____

_____

_____

_____

_____

_____

_____

_____

"IF ANYONE WOULD COME AFTER ME, LET HIM DENY HIMSELF
AND TAKE UP HIS CROSS AND FOLLOW ME."

MATTHEW 16:24

THE WORD OF THE LORD IS RIGHT AND TRUE;
HE IS FAITHFUL IN ALL HE DOES.

PSALM 33:4

THE LORD IS MY STRENGTH AND MY SHIELD;
MY HEART TRUSTS IN HIM, AND HE HELPS ME.

PSALM 28:7

IN HIM WE HAVE REDEMPTION THROUGH HIS BLOOD,
THE FORGIVENESS OF SINS, IN ACCORDANCE
WITH THE RICHES OF GOD'S GRACE. EPHESIANS 1:7

_____

_____

_____

_____

_____

_____

_____

_____

_____

_____

_____

_____

_____

_____

_____

_____

_____

_____

_____

_____

_____

I TRUST IN YOUR UNFAILING LOVE. I WILL REJOICE
BECAUSE YOU HAVE RESCUED ME. I WILL SING TO
THE LORD BECAUSE HE IS SO GOOD TO ME. PSALM 13:5-6

_____

_____

_____

_____

_____

_____

_____

_____

_____

_____

_____

_____

_____

_____

_____

_____

_____

_____

_____

_____

_____

_____

WALK IN THE WAY OF LOVE, JUST AS CHRIST LOVED US
AND GAVE HIMSELF UP FOR US AS A FRAGRANT
OFFERING AND SACRIFICE TO GOD. EPHESIANS 5:2

_____

_____

_____

_____

_____

_____

_____

_____

_____

_____

_____

_____

_____

_____

_____

_____

_____

_____

_____

_____

_____

"YOU WILL CALL UPON ME AND COME AND PRAY TO ME, AND I WILL
LISTEN TO YOU. YOU WILL SEEK ME AND FIND ME WHEN
YOU SEEK ME WITH ALL YOUR HEART." JEREMIAH 29:12-13

MY SOUL FINDS REST IN GOD; MY SALVATION COMES FROM HIM.

PSALM 62:1

DELIGHT YOURSELF IN THE LORD,
AND HE WILL GIVE YOU THE DESIRES OF YOUR HEART.

PSALM 37:4

THE LORD IS MY LIGHT AND MY SALVATION—
WHOM SHALL I FEAR? THE LORD IS THE STRONGHOLD OF
MY LIFE—OF WHOM SHALL I BE AFRAID? PSALM 27:1

THE LORD HIMSELF GOES BEFORE YOU AND WILL BE WITH YOU;
HE WILL NEVER LEAVE YOU NOR FORSAKE YOU.

DEUTERONOMY 31:8

_____

_____

_____

_____

_____

_____

_____

_____

_____

_____

_____

_____

_____

_____

_____

_____

_____

_____

_____

_____

_____

_____

_____

GOD IS WORKING IN YOU, GIVING YOU THE DESIRE
TO OBEY HIM AND THE POWER TO DO WHAT PLEASES HIM.

PHILIPPIANS 2:13

I CAN DO EVERYTHING THROUGH CHRIST, WHO GIVES ME STRENGTH.

PHILIPPIANS 4:13

IF YOU WANT TO KNOW WHAT GOD WANTS YOU TO DO,
ASK HIM, AND HE WILL GLADLY TELL YOU.

JAMES 1:5

CREATE IN ME A PURE HEART, O GOD,
AND RENEW A STEADFAST SPIRIT WITHIN ME.

PSALM 51:10

IF ANYONE IS IN CHRIST, THE NEW CREATION HAS COME:
THE OLD HAS GONE, THE NEW IS HERE!

2 CORINTHIANS 5:17

CAST YOUR CARES ON THE LORD AND HE WILL SUSTAIN YOU.

PSALM 55:22

THE LORD YOUR GOD IS WITH YOU, THE MIGHTY WARRIOR WHO SAVES. HE WILL
TAKE GREAT DELIGHT IN YOU; IN HIS LOVE HE WILL NO LONGER REBUKE YOU.

ZEPHANIAH 3:17

THE LORD IS TRUSTWORTHY IN ALL HE
PROMISES AND FAITHFUL IN ALL HE DOES.

PSALM 145:13

IN YOU, O LORD, DO I TAKE REFUGE;
LET ME NEVER BE PUT TO SHAME!

PSALM 71:1

"BE STRONG AND COURAGEOUS . . . THE LORD YOUR GOD
WILL BE WITH YOU WHEREVER YOU GO."

JOSHUA 1:9

COMMIT TO THE LORD WHATEVER YOU DO,
AND HE WILL ESTABLISH YOUR PLANS.

PROVERBS 16:3

SINCE WE HAVE BEEN JUSTIFIED THROUGH FAITH,
WE HAVE PEACE WITH GOD THROUGH OUR LORD JESUS CHRIST.

ROMANS 5:1

THE LORD IS MY ROCK, MY FORTRESS AND MY DELIVERER;
MY GOD IS MY ROCK, IN WHOM I TAKE REFUGE.

PSALM 18:2

_____

_____

_____

_____

_____

_____

_____

_____

_____

_____

_____

_____

_____

_____

_____

_____

_____

_____

_____

_____

_____

_____

_____

_____

"IF ANYONE WOULD COME AFTER ME, LET HIM DENY HIMSELF
AND TAKE UP HIS CROSS AND FOLLOW ME."

MATTHEW 16:24

THE WORD OF THE LORD IS RIGHT AND TRUE;
HE IS FAITHFUL IN ALL HE DOES.

PSALM 33:4

THE LORD IS MY STRENGTH AND MY SHIELD;
MY HEART TRUSTS IN HIM, AND HE HELPS ME.

PSALM 28:7

IN HIM WE HAVE REDEMPTION THROUGH HIS BLOOD,
THE FORGIVENESS OF SINS, IN ACCORDANCE
WITH THE RICHES OF GOD'S GRACE. EPHESIANS 1:7

_____

_____

_____

_____

_____

_____

_____

_____

_____

_____

_____

_____

_____

_____

_____

_____

_____

_____

_____

_____

_____

_____

_____

_____

I TRUST IN YOUR UNFAILING LOVE. I WILL REJOICE
BECAUSE YOU HAVE RESCUED ME. I WILL SING TO
THE LORD BECAUSE HE IS SO GOOD TO ME. PSALM 13:5-6

WALK IN THE WAY OF LOVE, JUST AS CHRIST LOVED US
AND GAVE HIMSELF UP FOR US AS A FRAGRANT
OFFERING AND SACRIFICE TO GOD. EPHESIANS 5:2

"YOU WILL CALL UPON ME AND COME AND PRAY TO ME, AND I WILL
LISTEN TO YOU. YOU WILL SEEK ME AND FIND ME WHEN
YOU SEEK ME WITH ALL YOUR HEART." JEREMIAH 29:12-13

MY SOUL FINDS REST IN GOD; MY SALVATION COMES FROM HIM.

PSALM 62:1

_____

_____

_____

_____

_____

_____

_____

_____

_____

_____

_____

_____

_____

_____

_____

_____

_____

_____

_____

_____

_____

_____

DELIGHT YOURSELF IN THE LORD,
AND HE WILL GIVE YOU THE DESIRES OF YOUR HEART.

PSALM 37:4

_____

_____

_____

_____

_____

_____

_____

_____

_____

_____

_____

_____

_____

_____

_____

_____

_____

_____

_____

_____

_____

_____

_____

THE LORD IS MY LIGHT AND MY SALVATION—
WHOM SHALL I FEAR? THE LORD IS THE STRONGHOLD OF
MY LIFE—OF WHOM SHALL I BE AFRAID? PSALM 27:1

THE LORD HIMSELF GOES BEFORE YOU AND WILL BE WITH YOU;
HE WILL NEVER LEAVE YOU NOR FORSAKE YOU.

DEUTERONOMY 31:8

GOD IS WORKING IN YOU, GIVING YOU THE DESIRE
TO OBEY HIM AND THE POWER TO DO WHAT PLEASES HIM.

PHILIPPIANS 2:13

I CAN DO EVERYTHING THROUGH CHRIST, WHO GIVES ME STRENGTH.

PHILIPPIANS 4:13

_____

_____

_____

_____

_____

_____

_____

_____

_____

_____

_____

_____

_____

_____

_____

_____

_____

_____

_____

_____

_____

_____

_____

_____

_____

_____

IF YOU WANT TO KNOW WHAT GOD WANTS YOU TO DO,
ASK HIM, AND HE WILL GLADLY TELL YOU.

JAMES 1:5

CREATE IN ME A PURE HEART, O GOD,
AND RENEW A STEADFAST SPIRIT WITHIN ME.

PSALM 51:10

IF ANYONE IS IN CHRIST, THE NEW CREATION HAS COME:
THE OLD HAS GONE, THE NEW IS HERE!

2 CORINTHIANS 5:17

CAST YOUR CARES ON THE LORD AND HE WILL SUSTAIN YOU.

THE LORD YOUR GOD IS WITH YOU, THE MIGHTY WARRIOR WHO SAVES. HE WILL
TAKE GREAT DELIGHT IN YOU; IN HIS LOVE HE WILL NO LONGER REBUKE YOU.

ZEPHANIAH 3:17

THE LORD IS TRUSTWORTHY IN ALL HE
PROMISES AND FAITHFUL IN ALL HE DOES.

PSALM 145:13

IN YOU, O LORD, DO I TAKE REFUGE;
LET ME NEVER BE PUT TO SHAME!

PSALM 71:1

_____

_____

_____

_____

_____

_____

_____

_____

_____

_____

_____

_____

_____

_____

_____

_____

_____

_____

_____

_____

_____

_____

_____

"BE STRONG AND COURAGEOUS . . . THE LORD YOUR GOD
WILL BE WITH YOU WHEREVER YOU GO."

JOSHUA 1:9

COMMIT TO THE LORD WHATEVER YOU DO,
AND HE WILL ESTABLISH YOUR PLANS.

PROVERBS 16:3

SINCE WE HAVE BEEN JUSTIFIED THROUGH FAITH,
WE HAVE PEACE WITH GOD THROUGH OUR LORD JESUS CHRIST.

ROMANS 5:1

THE LORD IS MY ROCK, MY FORTRESS AND MY DELIVERER;
MY GOD IS MY ROCK, IN WHOM I TAKE REFUGE.

PSALM 18:2

"IF ANYONE WOULD COME AFTER ME, LET HIM DENY HIMSELF
AND TAKE UP HIS CROSS AND FOLLOW ME."

MATTHEW 16:24

THE WORD OF THE LORD IS RIGHT AND TRUE;
HE IS FAITHFUL IN ALL HE DOES.

PSALM 33:4

THE LORD IS MY STRENGTH AND MY SHIELD;
MY HEART TRUSTS IN HIM, AND HE HELPS ME.

PSALM 28:7

IN HIM WE HAVE REDEMPTION THROUGH HIS BLOOD,
THE FORGIVENESS OF SINS, IN ACCORDANCE
WITH THE RICHES OF GOD'S GRACE. EPHESIANS 1:7

I TRUST IN YOUR UNFAILING LOVE. I WILL REJOICE
BECAUSE YOU HAVE RESCUED ME. I WILL SING TO
THE LORD BECAUSE HE IS SO GOOD TO ME. PSALM 13:5-6

WALK IN THE WAY OF LOVE, JUST AS CHRIST LOVED US
AND GAVE HIMSELF UP FOR US AS A FRAGRANT
OFFERING AND SACRIFICE TO GOD. EPHESIANS 5:2

_____

_____

_____

_____

_____

_____

_____

_____

_____

_____

_____

_____

_____

_____

_____

_____

_____

_____

_____

_____

_____

"YOU WILL CALL UPON ME AND COME AND PRAY TO ME, AND I WILL
LISTEN TO YOU. YOU WILL SEEK ME AND FIND ME WHEN
YOU SEEK ME WITH ALL YOUR HEART." JEREMIAH 29:12-13

MY SOUL FINDS REST IN GOD; MY SALVATION COMES FROM HIM.

PSALM 62:1

DELIGHT YOURSELF IN THE LORD,
AND HE WILL GIVE YOU THE DESIRES OF YOUR HEART.

PSALM 37:4

THE LORD IS MY LIGHT AND MY SALVATION—
WHOM SHALL I FEAR? THE LORD IS THE STRONGHOLD OF
MY LIFE—OF WHOM SHALL I BE AFRAID? PSALM 27:1

THE LORD HIMSELF GOES BEFORE YOU AND WILL BE WITH YOU;
HE WILL NEVER LEAVE YOU NOR FORSAKE YOU.

DEUTERONOMY 31:8

_____

_____

_____

_____

_____

_____

_____

_____

_____

_____

_____

_____

_____

_____

_____

_____

_____

_____

_____

_____

_____

_____

GOD IS WORKING IN YOU, GIVING YOU THE DESIRE
TO OBEY HIM AND THE POWER TO DO WHAT PLEASES HIM.

PHILIPPIANS 2:13

I CAN DO EVERYTHING THROUGH CHRIST, WHO GIVES ME STRENGTH.

PHILIPPIANS 4:13

_____
_____
_____
_____
_____
_____
_____
_____
_____
_____
_____
_____
_____
_____
_____
_____
_____
_____
_____
_____
_____
_____
_____

IF YOU WANT TO KNOW WHAT GOD WANTS YOU TO DO,
ASK HIM, AND HE WILL GLADLY TELL YOU.

JAMES 1:5

CREATE IN ME A PURE HEART, O GOD,
AND RENEW A STEADFAST SPIRIT WITHIN ME.

PSALM 51:10

_____

_____

_____

_____

_____

_____

_____

_____

_____

_____

_____

_____

_____

_____

_____

_____

_____

_____

_____

_____

_____

_____

IF ANYONE IS IN CHRIST, THE NEW CREATION HAS COME:
THE OLD HAS GONE, THE NEW IS HERE!

2 CORINTHIANS 5:17

CAST YOUR CARES ON THE LORD AND HE WILL SUSTAIN YOU.

_____

_____

_____

_____

_____

_____

_____

_____

_____

_____

_____

_____

_____

_____

_____

_____

_____

_____

_____

_____

_____

_____

THE LORD YOUR GOD IS WITH YOU, THE MIGHTY WARRIOR WHO SAVES. HE WILL
TAKE GREAT DELIGHT IN YOU; IN HIS LOVE HE WILL NO LONGER REBUKE YOU.

ZEPHANIAH 3:17

THE LORD IS TRUSTWORTHY IN ALL HE
PROMISES AND FAITHFUL IN ALL HE DOES.

PSALM 145:13

IN YOU, O LORD, DO I TAKE REFUGE;
LET ME NEVER BE PUT TO SHAME!

PSALM 71:1

"BE STRONG AND COURAGEOUS . . . THE LORD YOUR GOD
WILL BE WITH YOU WHEREVER YOU GO."

JOSHUA 1:9

COMMIT TO THE LORD WHATEVER YOU DO,
AND HE WILL ESTABLISH YOUR PLANS.

PROVERBS 16:3

SINCE WE HAVE BEEN JUSTIFIED THROUGH FAITH,
WE HAVE PEACE WITH GOD THROUGH OUR LORD JESUS CHRIST.

ROMANS 5:1

THE LORD IS MY ROCK, MY FORTRESS AND MY DELIVERER;
MY GOD IS MY ROCK, IN WHOM I TAKE REFUGE.

PSALM 18:2

_____

_____

_____

_____

_____

_____

_____

_____

_____

_____

_____

_____

_____

_____

_____

_____

_____

_____

_____

_____

_____

_____

_____

"IF ANYONE WOULD COME AFTER ME, LET HIM DENY HIMSELF
AND TAKE UP HIS CROSS AND FOLLOW ME."

MATTHEW 16:24

THE WORD OF THE LORD IS RIGHT AND TRUE;
HE IS FAITHFUL IN ALL HE DOES.

PSALM 33:4

THE LORD IS MY STRENGTH AND MY SHIELD;
MY HEART TRUSTS IN HIM, AND HE HELPS ME.

PSALM 28:7

IN HIM WE HAVE REDEMPTION THROUGH HIS BLOOD,
THE FORGIVENESS OF SINS, IN ACCORDANCE
WITH THE RICHES OF GOD'S GRACE. EPHESIANS 1:7

I TRUST IN YOUR UNFAILING LOVE. I WILL REJOICE
BECAUSE YOU HAVE RESCUED ME. I WILL SING TO
THE LORD BECAUSE HE IS SO GOOD TO ME. PSALM 13:5-6

WALK IN THE WAY OF LOVE, JUST AS CHRIST LOVED US
AND GAVE HIMSELF UP FOR US AS A FRAGRANT
OFFERING AND SACRIFICE TO GOD. EPHESIANS 5:2